# Success~~ful~~
# Web sites
# in a week

## STEVE MORRIS
## PAUL DICKINSON

# Hodder & Stoughton

A MEMBER OF THE HODDER HEADLINE GROUP

Order queries: please contact Bookpoint Ltd, 39 Milton Park, Abingdon, Oxon
OX14 4TD. Telephone: (44) 01235 400414, Fax: (44) 01235 400454. Lines are
open from 9.00 - 6.00, Monday to Saturday, with a 24 hour message answering
service. Email address: orders@bookpoint.co.uk

*British Library Cataloguing in Publication Data*
A catalogue record for this title is available from The British Library

ISBN 0 340 70508 6

First published 1998
Impression number    10  9  8  7  6  5  4  3  2  1
Year                 2003  2002  2001  2000  1999  1998

Typeset by Multiplex Techniques Ltd, St Mary Cray, Kent.
Printed in Great Britain for Hodder & Stoughton Educational, a division of
Hodder Headline Plc, 338 Euston Road, London NW1 3BH by Cox and
Wyman, Reading, Berkshire.

**the Institute of Management**

*FOUNDATION*

The Institute of Management (IM) exists to promote the development, exercise and recognition of professional management. The Institute embraces all levels of management from student to chief executive and supports its own Foundation which provides a unique portfolio of services for all managers, enabling them to develop skills and achieve management excellence.

For information on the various levels and benefits of membership, please contact:

Department HS
Institute of Management
Cottingham Road
Corby
Northants NN17 1TT
Tel: 01536 204222
Fax: 01536 201651

This series is commissioned by the Institute of Management Foundation.

# CONTENTS

The Internet has been around for a long time, but in the last two years it has become an indispensable tool for all businesses both big and small. The easy-to-use graphical part of the Internet is called the World Wide Web. In the near future, every sensible company in the world, and millions of individuals, will have a 'Web site'. Why?

The Internet is many different things, and it is changing and growing all the time – you could talk about it forever. But right now, the most important thing to remember is that it is the biggest version of Yellow Pages there has ever been in all history! Estimates vary but there are at least 500 million Internet pages available. These are also usually kept up to date, some by the month, others by the minute.

A small French flag-making company put up a Web page some years ago. When the planners for the Atlanta Olympics went looking for flag manufacturers on the Internet, this company got the biggest order of its life.

All the Web pages in the world are held in different places geographically, but the Internet changes that. When you connect to the Internet you can see any page, anywhere in the world, with equal ease and speed for the same price. The combination of all the content on the Internet, from all over the world, being made equally available to you on your computer is sometimes called 'Cyberspace' – because the information is not here or there but everywhere.

So, as most people in the world are making their business connections over the Internet, you need to be there too. This book aims to help you develop a successful Web site at work. It explains the process you can go through to deliver a successful Web site, the people to involve and some of the technical issues. A word of caution, though, before we begin. The world of Web sites is rapidly advancing and new ideas and solutions are being found all the time. In such a fast-changing world, you need to keep abreast of all the latest developments. One thing we do believe is that developing a Web site is as much an art as it is a science. So this book does not follow a simple scientific structure and formula. The Web is free-flowing and organic, and so is this book.

What is true is that there are about as many different ways to put together a Web site as there are Web sites! Very broadly, though, putting together any company Web site requires:

- Strategic thinking
- Planning
- Structuring
- Designing
- Writing
- Testing
- Launching, and
- Maintaining

| | |
|---|---|
| **Sunday** | Start with the thinking |
| **Monday** | Key concepts, users and uses |
| **Tuesday** | Assembling the site content |
| **Wednesday** | Planning and registering the sites, and choosing the production personnel |
| **Thursday** | The detailed work |
| **Friday** | Testing and launching the site |
| **Saturday** | Further possibilities |

# Start with the thinking

Today, you will start up by thinking through some of the strategic issues relating to Web sites. It is all too easy to dive into the detail, but without some good strategic thinking it is likely you'll run into problems with your Web site as you develop it.

The first thing to do today is to start thinking through some broad issues and questions. Although developing a Web site seems whizzy and exciting, it does need careful and clear-headed strategic thought. There are a range of broad issues and questions to consider.

## What do you want the Web site to do?

All too often, companies have jumped into developing a Web site without thinking through what they want it to do and, indeed, how they will measure its success. In some instances, developing a Web site has been a case of Keeping Up With The Joneses: if they've got one, we'd better have one. Although in some senses it is important to keep up with the competition, you do need to think more profoundly. Ask yourself the following questions:

*Why are we embarking on developing a Web site?*
Are there sound business reasons for doing so? If there are, what are they? If there are not, should you delay?

A couple of useful questions to consider here are:

- Will you be able to make savings on conventional printing and distribution by using your Web site? It is sometimes the case that Web sites can save money over conventional media
- What would you want to see on a Web site? How much will it cost to realise your dreams?

It is best to develop a business case by thinking in terms of savings with regard to advertising, promotion and communications combined with improved 'marketing' to, and communication with, customers. If you compare the Internet to the telephone, few businesses ask themselves how much money they make on the 'phone each day, but all agree it is an essential medium.

*Is the Web site going to make a major corporate statement?*
If so, it is likely to be a major exercise involving great time and expense and a range of leading stakeholders in the company.

*Do we want a Web site mainly to tell people about us, or are we going to use it to receive information, or perhaps orders, from customers too?*

If you want to use your Web site to receive information, then you are going to have to really work to make it interactive. If you are going to use it to sell things, then there are going to be technical issues you'll need to address.

Because the Internet is a fast-evolving and ever-changing medium, it is particularly important to decide what you want to get out of it. That way you can avoid lots of unnecessary expense and get the site right first time.

You will look in more detail at the different types of Web site tomorrow.

*What resources is the company or organisation prepared to commit?*
Tens of thousands of Web sites have foundered on the rocks of finance and project management. This is therefore a really important strategic question, and one, again, that is often ignored in the desire to get started in the big exciting world of Web sites.

Lots of things about developing and maintaining a site require resources. The human resources can be both internal and external. And there are also always development costs. The faster you want the site to download, the more the technical development is likely to cost.

*What people need to be involved?*
Will you need external help, or can a project team from within the organisation do all the work? If you need people from outside, do you have commissioning experience? If not, how can you make sure you get a good reliable firm and not a bunch of Wyatt Earps from down the road? You are certainly going to need to think through the wider project team.

Just some of the people who are likely to be needed are:

- Designers
- Writers
- Programmers
- Project managers
- Content experts

*Do you have a clear idea of how your Web site will fit into your broader communications strategy?*
You need to be sure that developing the site won't take emphasis away from the rest of your communications. If you have strong brand values and identities, how will your Web site fit in with this?

It would be foolish, not to say disastrous, to develop a Web site that is completely out of line with all your other communications and not tied in with your organisation's wider strategies and positioning. Here are just a few areas to get you thinking:

What do you say, how do you say it, and to whom? Are you a pressure group trying to save the world, or a manufacturer of helmets for the Fire Service? Your audience might be very wide or very narrow. Consider geography. Will you create different-language versions of your site?

How should your Internet site work with your telephone sales people? On the page describing products, should the text read 'Call us now on 01234 56789 to order this item.'? If so, your call reception people should have access to the Web site too. Conversely, make sure that when people telephone and ask for a brochure, you offer them your Web site. They may prefer to access the information that way, and it may well save you money in printing and postage.

Does your organisation have a major requirement to communicate a lot of information to a particular audience? For example, if your business involves running a number of franchisees, would it make sense to offer them all the information they need from your Web site, rather than sending out great bulky manuals that go out of date? Would you want to include a password function to stop competitors viewing some of your information? In this context, an on-line chartroom would be an excellent means for franchisees to share experiences and develop best practice.

*How will the site be maintained, supported and updated?*
To get people to revisit the site, it is necessary to refresh the information on it. This takes time and involves costs. Have you decided whether you can afford to update and maintain the site? Recent figures have shown that all too often companies don't think this issue through. There are simply millions of what are known as 'cobweb sites' on the World Wide Web: sites that are unloved and unupdated and consequently unvisited.

Perhaps leave yourself the following memo to remind
yourself of the task ahead:

*Please detail any content you wish to include on the site.*
*Remember that any content will have to be kept up to date by you*
*forever in the future!*

This gives some sense of the size of the updating task.
Remember, because the Internet is 'live', things do not go
out of date between issues: they go out of date instantly.

*When is the site really needed by?*
Unlike other communication mediums, Web sites seem
always to be done in a rush. Perhaps it is the excitement
they evoke. Perhaps it is the feeling that companies want to
get a presence quickly and not be left behind. Whatever the
cause, this rush and hurry tends to lead to great stress for
those tasked with developing the site, and often quite
unrealistic deadlines – developing a Web site does take
time. So ask yourself when the site is really needed by.

*What political and practical support will you need?*
Developing a Web site can be a hard slog, fraught with
unexpected technical problems, delays and cost overruns.
It can also be quite political: the way the company presents
itself on the Internet is likely to generate much heat and
debate. So if you are involved in developing a Web site, do
you feel you have the real support and back-up from within
your organisation that you will need if the going gets tough?

*How leading-edge do you want to be?*
There are plenty of guys with pony tails who promise the
earth, but just how leading-edge do you want to be? Can
you afford the technical development and time it takes to
be leading-edge? Can you afford not to be leading-edge?

*What can you learn from other sites?*
Before you plan in detail, familiarise yourself with the
Internet, look at what is out there and gain ideas. The thing
about the Internet is that it is visible: you don't have to
hunt around dusty old libraries in order to gather ideas for
your Web site.

Because this is only Sunday, if you do not have your own
Internet connection at home, you can easily visit one of the
hundreds of 'Internet cafés' in the UK, but try to telephone
first to check that they have a fast Internet connection. The
best way to learn about Internet communications is by
example. Many thousands of companies have already spent
enormous time and effort to develop sites, so make notes of
what seems to work well and pay particular attention to
how easy it is to find your way around the site – i.e.
'navigation', as it is known in the Web site world. Make
notes about what you do and don't like about the sites
you visit.

It may be helpful to prepare a table of categories which you can use to judge the Internet sites you visit against. Try giving each site marks out of 10. Typically, the areas you would review might include the following:

1   What were the objectives of the site?
2   Does it download quickly?
3   Do the pages download in a sensible sequence?
4   Is it interesting to visit?
5   Are the graphics relevant and attractive?
6   Is the site well-written – is it lively and interesting?
7   Is it full of relevant content?
8   Is it being kept up to date?
9   Does it reflect the character of the organisation?
10  Is it easy to navigate and use the site?

   – Is the content structured logically?
   – Is it easy to find what you want?
   – Did you ever get 'lost' on the site?
   – Did it take forever to 'click' to where you wanted to go?
   – Are there too many or too few levels of information?
   – Is there a good 'local' search engine? (A 'local' search engine searches only on the Web site you are visiting.)
   – How are the 'Frames' used (Frames are a device which creates separate panels on the screen which do not all change when you move from page to page.) Are they effective?

11  Overall, is the site a success?

Look at Web pages for telephone companies, computer companies, TV companies and travel companies because these organisations usually spend a lot of time and effort on their Internet sites. Some good examples include:

> http://www.cnn.com
> http://www.microsoft.com
> http://www.ibm.com
> http://www.bt.com
> http://www.sky.co.uk
> http://www.sony.com
> http://www.dell.com
> http://www.railtrack.co.uk

At the same time, have a look at a range of other kinds of company and organisation. Try to spend a few hours familiarising yourself with the extraordinary diversity of Internet communications.

## Summary

Today, you have looked at some of the broad issues and strategic issues about Web sites. You have also completed a competitor analysis. The research phase continues tomorrow.

# Key concepts, users and uses

Today is about familiarising yourself with some key concepts, researching your audiences, choosing what your Web site can do for you, and making some detailed plans.

## The key concepts

As you go about researching the Internet and feeling comfortable in cyberspace, you will need to understand three main areas:

1 HyperText links
2 Uniform Resource Locations (URLs)
  (the name of an Internet site)
3 Search engines

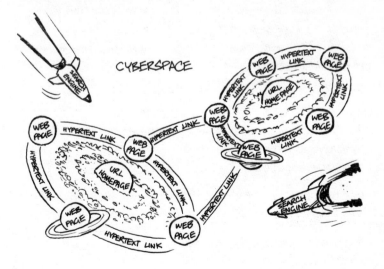

These sound dreadful but they are not as complicated as they sound. In many ways, these three areas are at the heart of most successful Web sites.

*HyperText links*
The World Wide Web is based on 'HyperText Markup Language' or 'HTML'. The 'HyperText' part of the name is one of the best things about the Internet. Whenever you click your mouse on a word which is underlined, or a linked graphic, you fly away to the particular Web page to which it is connected. One of the most important secrets of a successful Web site is to be visited by people. So, thinking through links and linkages is a key first step in any Web site.

*URLs, or How will people look for your Web site?*
This is a very important question. With 500 million Web pages, and possibly many more, finding your way around is very difficult. The easiest way is by using Internet naming conventions. These work very well for big companies. Rather than explain, below are listed five big company Web addresses or URLs. The system is sometimes easy to understand:

| | |
|---|---|
| http://www.bt.com | British Telecommunications |
| http://www.bp.com | British Petroleum |
| http://www.shell.com | Shell International Petroleum |
| http://www.ibm.com | IBM |
| http://www.apple.com | Apple Computer |

However, this system does fall apart sometimes! Would Rolls Royce be:

| | |
|---|---|
| http://www.rolls-royce.com | or |
| http://www.rolls_royce.com | or |
| http://www.rollsroyce.com | or |

http://www.rollsroyce.co.uk     or any one of a thousand others!

And there are two completely separate companies in the UK called Rolls Royce, one making aero engines and the other making cars.

Furthermore, there is more than one suffix naming convention for Internet sites, including:

| | |
|---|---|
| .com | for large North American or global companies |
| .co.uk | for UK companies |
| .org | for non-commercial organisations |
| .gov | for government sites |

…and many others. In addition, the conventions are growing and changing and evolving all the time. But, the advantage of having a simple URL which people will think of instinctively is that it avoids the need for 'search engines' (see next page), which can be troublesome.

The beauty of a URL is that it is your shopfront to the world. You don't have to fight for a prime sight on the high street. Your URL is your one global location!

*Search engines*

There are a range of these which work in slightly different ways, and some are better than others, but the basic idea is simple. On the browse you use to search the Internet, there will be a button called 'Search' or 'Net Search'. When you click on this, you will be offered a range of search engines with names such as 'Yahoo!', 'Alta Vista', 'Infoseek' and 'Excite'. When you have selected a search engine, you simply type in what you are looking for and the search engine then checks through vast databases of everything on the Internet.

This sounds easy. However, there is a problem. Imagine you wanted to find the 'Home Page' for Shell International Petroleum. If you type in 'Shell', you might find there are 500,000 Web pages featuring the word 'Shell', so what do you do? By following the instructions on the advanced search engine in Alta Vista, you could probably find Shell quite quickly. But what would you do if you don't know what you want?

This is where the real art of Internet communications comes into play. For example, say you have a broken window and you need a glazier, what do you do? If you do a search under 'Broken Window', who knows what you might find – probably nothing of any use. However, if you understand how the search engines work, and you understand how your customers think, it is possible to help your customers to find you.

Search engines work by regularly searching the entire Internet and recording the first, say, 50 words of every Web site. This text database is then searched by the search engine when you click 'Search'. It is possible to make the first 50 words of your site invisible so that only search engines can see them. This can help you to rise to the top of the list when people search for your site. However, a word

of warning! Imagine you are a glazier in London, and you make the first 50 invisible words of your site read: 'London Glazier London Glazier London Glazier London Glazier ...' etc. You will be hoping that anyone who runs a search under 'London' and 'Glazier' will get your site at the top of the search-results list. However, you should be warned! Most search engines now run 'de-duplication' packages which stop people sneaking to the top of the list like this. By all means try to weight searches in your favour by using certain words, but try not to duplicate!

Some search engines work by dividing information into categories, which allows the user to find all the sites relating to, for example, films all in one place. To appear in the categories you want to appear in, it is helpful to register with the relevant search engines. You may prefer to get a specialist company to do this for you.

Going back to the above example, perhaps there is an Internet address called:

http://www.glazier.com

Would someone with a broken window look there first? If there is such a site, it will probably be in the USA, as most Internet pages are in the USA. So maybe you should have inserted the name:

http://www.glazier.co.uk

or maybe there is a directory of UK Glaziers at:

http://www.glaziers.co.uk

These naming and searching issues will be less important if you simply anticipate giving people your URL by post or telephone and getting them to go straight to your site. But if you expect people to go out and find you, these issues will be particularly important.

*Action point*
Spend some time thinking of how your customers look for you and find you. Where do they come from, and what is on their minds when they start looking?

So that takes care of some key concepts. It is now time to go back to some more thinking and planning.

## First, understand your audiences

The next stage of the process should begin with serious research into your audiences. Web sites only work if they work with your audience. If your audience likes the Web site, it will keep on visiting. If not, you'll have a cobweb-strewn site that no-one likes.

*Do some research into customer preferences*
Take time to contact customers, suppliers and friends to find out what they would want to see on your Web site and how they would look for you. It is difficult for them to answer questions in a vacuum, so you could gently prompt them by saying:

'What are the 10 things you most often want to know when you telephone us?'
'What do we send you through the post which is most useful?'
'What parts of our business would you like to know more about?'

Keep a record of your findings. They will act as a useful backdrop to your more detailed Web-site development.

## Then, decide what your Web site can do for you

The next step is to start gathering ideas from the world of cyberspace to help you to develop your own site. The following are ideas to choose from as to what your Web site can do for you.

## 1 Boosting sales

There are some startling examples of businesses making millions by 'selling' over the Internet, but they tend to be the exceptions rather than the rule. However, there are no real barriers to selling over the Internet if you run an appropriate and relevant business and are committed to making it a success. What you need to do is make the medium work for you. Some businesses are better suited than others. For example, if you run a sweetshop, selling over the Internet might not make much sense because sweets are almost always bought with cash, and they tend to be demanded by hungry children who will not wait for them to arrive by post. However, if you are a sweets manufacturer selling to a number of wholesalers, the Internet might be just the right thing for you. This is because you would not tend to require cash to fulfil orders, and because you would know exactly whom you were delivering to. And the beauty of the Internet here is that it could cut out a tremendous amount of paperwork for you.

If you wanted to really make use of the medium, the only limit is your imagination. When selling sweets to wholesalers, would you include on your site an electronic 'shopping basket' that fills up with orders and calculates the total expenditure – and discount – automatically, and maybe even initiates an order? It is relatively straightforward to embed some form of calculator into your Web site. Would this help to improve the experience for your audience? Naturally, you would have to ensure that passwords and other security features protect you from malicious or false orders, but clearly the potential is vast.

## 2 Offering specialist services and knowledge

Would you want your site to offer the ability to 'tailor' the site content to suit the specific needs of different audiences? So, if I have a business which sells cars and car parts, would I present these two sides of the business differently, with more sales emphasis on the cars, and more functional emphasis on the parts?

## 3 Advertising and sponsorship

Do you plan to sell advertising on your site? If so, be warned: this may be very difficult. This is because the Internet delivers exact information regarding how many users visit your site, and advertisers' expectations will be very high. A visit to a page is called a 'hit', and the number of 'hits' achieved by a Web site tends to be the chief measure of its popularity. All Web sites get a few hundred hits. This is because a certain number of hits are generated 'automatically' by search engines. So to actually sell some advertising, you will have to prove that thousands of real people are visiting you. Would you be able to do that? In addition, graphics slow the Internet down, so do you want to make your site slow for your customers, just so that someone can advertise to them?

Sponsorship might, however, be a simpler option as sponsors will probably not require a definite 'bottom line' output for their contribution in the same way as will advertisers. If you provide a site showing information about old buildings in your area, would an estate agent or other local business be prepared to sponsor the site? In this sense, advertising and sponsorship are similar, but it is probably easier to manage your backers' expectations through sponsorship.

## 4 Incentives

Can you offer prizes to try to keep people on your site? Prizes are often a wonderful way to collect information regarding visitors. The idea is that if a user of the Internet, or 'Web surfer', visits your site, you invite them to enter a competition free, in exchange for taking their details – name, company name, job title, area of interest, address, telephone, fax and e-mail number, etc. In this way, every entrant to your competition could become a sales lead, and is already entered into your database electronically. If you do offer a prize, call the surfer to action with a bold 'Click here to win so and so' button.

There are, however, some problems with competitions. For example, don't be surprised if half the contestants are school kids from the other side of the planet! Look out for 'Mr Willy Wonker, Chief Chocolate Manufacturer, Dingley Dell, Outer Space'.

*5 As publicity*
We have discussed Internet-based marketing, but what about direct mail, magazine advertising or even radio? The script could run as follows: 'For best-value prices and the biggest range, visit our Web site at www.myshop.co.uk.' You may also like to consider joining in newsgroups and chat forums relating to your particular area where you can tell people about your site.

If you want to build up a regular dialogue with customers or friends and you plan to keep your site regularly updated, you could consider asking visitors to sign up for an e-mail reminder service. This will take some time and money to configure, but once it is established, whenever you update the site you can automatically let your audience know of the improvements.

## Summary

At the end of Monday, you should have developed a good idea of what your customers, suppliers and friends would like to see from your Internet site. You should also have thought practically about what you can achieve in terms of time and resources. Finally, you should have covered some of the general issues and, at the end of this process, begun to develop the strategic plan for your Internet communications. Do not hurry this stage because planning is everything.

## Assembling the site content

Today, you start assembling the content for your site. This is an important job, because there is often a wealth of material to choose from. Get the balance and level of content right and your site is likely to work.

The golden rule here is to remember that this site is you. For a company, that means communicating at exactly the same level of quality as through your other media. Don't think that electronic media will disguise a mess: it won't. Instead, it will show a mess to the whole world! Get the best qualities of your identity or brand out on the Internet, because that is what sells you.

For a large company, developing a Web site is like opening a huge reception area to anyone who is passing by. You will need to involve every department to make sure they all have the chance to benefit from the Internet opportunity.

Would the sales department like to have brochures visible?
Would personnel like to have recruitment literature?

Look at all your existing literature and communications.
What can and should migrate to the Internet?

## Timing

This issue is also important. Does it make sense to try to
put everything you possibly can onto your Web site
straight away, or do you want to wait and see how much
use people are really making of the site? The ideal plan
probably involves you getting a simple site up early and
perhaps scheduling the arrival of content according to the
enthusiasm of departmental contributors! Alternatively, for
a more structured approach, make a list of priorities and
make sure the site develops according to this plan.

## Action point

Draw up a clear structure chart showing each area of the
site, the hierarchy of information and the logic behind it.
Talk it through with other people. Make sure it is right.
Structuring and presenting information effectively is
probably the most important aspect of Web-site design.

The end result is likely to be a detailed diagram of the site
content.

## Now work on the important features of a Web site

There are no strict rules regarding the contents of a Web site. Because you can communicate just about everything to everyone, care needs to be taken to ensure you don't end up with an unruly mess. Larger sites should be created directly from databases which will solve some of the problems of inconsistent format.

As a general guide, however, below are listed some of the main elements you will often find on a Web site. Think them through and it will help you to assemble the content that is right for your Web site.

*1 Home page*
Consider your home page very carefully. It is a combination of your front door, reception and corporate brochure. This is your big chance to 'sock it to them' and blast out what makes you special. Remember, first impressions count.

There are a number of questions to consider when planning the home page. For instance, what is the Unique Selling Point of your business? Make sure your unique character comes over straight away so the user is tempted to spend more time inside the site.

## 2 Company profile

For slightly larger organisations, it is always useful to include an organisational chart or structure chart. This is a very quick and easy way to show the strength and breadth of your capabilities and operations. This will provide an opportunity for your actual and prospective customers to consider working with all parts of your business.

Very often, organisations use their Web site to show their annual report and accounts, which also gives people an immediate sense of who they are and their financial strength. For public companies, this can also reduce the number of documents that need to be printed and sent out, which might result in considerable cost savings.

## 3 Press information

Press releases are often thought of as ideal content for an Internet site because they are urgent. The beauty of the Internet is that, the day you post information is the day it appears there: the Web is instant and global. If combined effectively with an e-mail programme to alert journalists, your Web site can easily become a key resource for communicating news about your organisation.

A word of warning, however. If you look at big company Web sites, you may find they usually contain the annual report and press releases and nothing more. This is a classic mistake caused by the fact that the Corporate Affairs department has generated the whole site on its own! Much better to involve all principal departments in a company to make sure the Web site reflects all your communications.

### 4 Recruitment

This is an area for which many companies feel the Internet is particularly well suited. Most bright graduates and other forward-thinking people in the job market will use the Internet to research companies and find jobs. Maybe one of your existing customers, or somebody just browsing, will apply for a job. If you have vacancies, make sure they are clearly signposted. Notice also that there are no recruitment agency fees!

### 5 Feedback

Include a section which encourages users to engage with you. Normally this is called 'Feedback', but maybe 'suggestions' is more your style, or even 'complaints'? Either way, you want to create a community based on interaction with your site, so work at this area.

### 6 Free gifts

It is great to be able to offer things on the Internet as a means of attracting and keeping visitors. Software which is free to all is called 'Freeware' and can be a super gift for people. Perhaps you would like to develop a screensaver full of jokes, poems, cartoons etc. which people can download. This is an excellent way to offer a permanent advert for your company. However, if you do pursue this route, take care to ensure that what you give away is completely bug-and copyright-free!

### 7 The potential for Intranets

If you have never heard of them before, you might believe that the above heading is a misprint. 'Intranets' are the name given to the Web sites a company uses internally which are not connected to the public Internet. Some companies such as GlaxoWellcome, have a large amount of their Internet information on Web sites which all their staff can access using Web browsers.

This information is confidential to GlaxoWellcome, so it is not possible to access it from the public Internet. It is protected from the Internet by a secure barrier called a 'firewall'.

For large companies, the public Internet is actually rather less important than their private intranets. We mention intranets here because all the above listed areas, i.e. organisational charts, recruitment, feedback and downloadable software, would all potentially be of equal interest to an internal company audience. With Internet technology, you don't have to publish this material twice as everything available on the public Internet can also be made available on the private internal intranet. This excellent feature of Web-based communications should be borne in mind when deciding what material to transfer to the Internet, and when carrying out a cost – benefit analysis of the process.

*8 Helping customers to buy from you*
This is perhaps the most exciting area of Internet communications and it needs plenty of thought. You need to start by putting yourself in your customers' shoes.

If you own a hotel, for example, think of the types of information a user is likely to want from you – for example, room rates, photos of rooms and views, local information and travel details. Perhaps you should also provide links to other Web sites that have local information of interest to your prospective customers. And don't ever forget to include a telephone contact number in case people want to book there and then. Or could you offer a facility to book a room directly over the Internet? If so, you will need to ensure your computer is constantly attended, just like the telephone.

### 9 Search engines

With the right search engine, every aspect of your Internet
site will be searchable. That means every word of text. This
can be a wonderful way to find information. You will need
to consider what kind of search you require. Would your
users like to have a very comprehensive search facility, or
would something very simple be more appropriate?

### 10 Video?

It is possible to show small video clips on your Web page,
but as you can imagine, these can take forever to download.
We would not recommend video unless your target
audience has high-speed ISDN telephone lines and good
computers. There is, however, a new technology called
'streaming' which can be used for video and audio, as
described below. This requires users to buy a player which
will cost them some money, but it allows people to watch
and download at the same time. We recommend you
thoroughly research these technologies in relevant computer
magazines before you consider these kinds of features.

*11 Sound and vision?*

It is also possible to use 'audio' on your Web site. Imagine that users visit your site to see and hear someone talk, or to hear music. Unfortunately, this requires the user to have a sound card fitted to their PC, combined with some specialist software, and not everybody has this. In addition, sound files – like video – are huge and therefore slow to communicate. However, use of 'multimedia' is definitely the future of the Internet. The way to conquer markets is to hit your customers' ears and eyes. Players are available for both audio and video.

Now go through the above list again and make a list of all the things you want your Web site to do for your organisation.

## An initial spec

At this point, you should be able to draw upon the planning done so far to begin to develop an initial technical specification. This should ideally include key information such as the byte size of pages and the functionality which you hope to include.

If you are not sufficiently familiar with the Internet to know what file size is acceptable, find a friend or Internet café where there is an 'average' computer and an 'average' modem. Probably the lowest-specification machine would be a 486 processor or better, with a 14.4 modem or better.

Spend time downloading pages from different companies, and familiarise yourself with the different time pages take to arrive. Notice that it often differs between morning and afternoon. In the afternoon, America wakes up and joins the Internet, slowing everybody down with congestion. When you have found what you consider to be an acceptable download time, study the size of the graphics on the page. This can be done by someone with technical savvy, or you could just telephone the relevant 'Webmaster' and ask.

## Summary

By the end of today, you should have gained a fairly clear idea of what you want the Web site to do for you and your organisation. You will also have started to think through some of the basic technical issues.

# Planning and registering the site, and choosing the production personnel

Today you will draw up a really structured plan for your site, register your site address and then decide who will actually produce the site itself.

## Begin by drawing up a structure chart

Begin by writing down all the different audiences you want to communicate with. These could include:

- Personal customers
- Business customers
- Researchers
- Suppliers
- Friends
- Prospective employees
- The media
- Prospective business partners
- Other stakeholders, governments, environmentalists etc.

Next, spend some time grouping together those users who have a common information requirement. Now you can begin the information-structuring process by highlighting those user groups on your draft 'Home page'.

Now it is time to begin sticking bits of paper on the wall! Consider carefully the 'journey' a user takes through your site. Think of how they will look for information, and anticipate their needs. Make sure that within each user group is everything they want, clearly labelled. There will be issues for you to resolve such as: is it better for people to 'drill down' into your site for information, or is it preferable to have long menus but only one or two levels of information? Try to draw on your experience of reviewing other people's sites to come up with the best solution for your audiences.

The end result here will be a detailed structure chart that will act as a map for your site. The chances are you'll have a map for your home page and then for every sub-section of the site, showing how the information drills down in detail. The map will act as a valuable reference as you go about collecting the detailed content and writing the site itself.

Drawing up the site map is likely to take time and to go through a number of revisions before everyone is comfortable with the shape of things. Brainstorm as many ideas as possible, and then begin to put them into a shape and structure. Think through the different levels of information and where different things will fit. Try not to be overwhelmed with detail at this stage. The idea is to come up with a skeleton on which you can hang the flesh later. Get everyone who has a stake in the Web site to take part in this exercise, and get as many ideas out into the open as possible.

To give an example, here is a Web site structure illustrating interview techniques. See how the different levels of detail are shown, as are the links between different parts of the site.

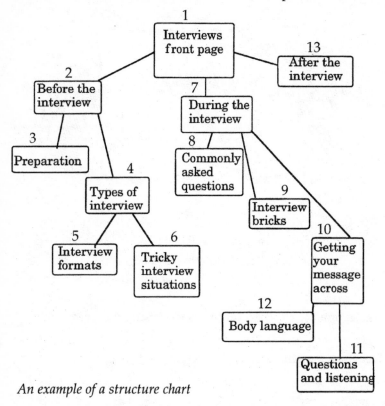

*An example of a structure chart*

## Register your URL

Don't spend too long choosing a name or somebody else might take it! You can check to see if the name you want is already taken by looking on the Internet at a name registration company, such as Netnames at 'http://www.netnames.co.uk'. Once you have selected your domain name, try very hard to stick to it. If you change your domain name in a year, and hundreds of other Web sites all have links to yours, these addresses will all become wrong.

## Choose a supplier, or do it yourself?

You've got your map and your URL. Now it is time to really get the development going. And any Web site development needs people to make it happen.

This process needs to be led by careful consideration of budget and available time. As a basic rule, don't spend all your money and effort in one go. Remember, you have to budget for management, maintenance and development of the site for a whole year, and you should also really be thinking of the years thereafter. Will you be keeping your site sufficiently up to date by changing it every month, or every week, or every day?

Be realistic about what you can achieve, and plan on that basis. If you can do things yourself, fine, but will you leave yourself exposed if you are confronted with difficult problems some time during the life of the project?

As part of your decision-making process, you will need to develop a clear sense of the scope of the task and the timescale you will be working to. These should then be set out to form the project plan which must be agreed by all parties involved in the development of the site.

*Action point*
The timetable should be realistic and carefully considered.
It must contain specific milestones and a fixed delivery
date. Don't let the project creep on later and later. Don't let
the ambitions for your Web site change and expand so
much that it can never be delivered. Get the site up by the
date you have set for yourself, whatever else may happen.

*Reviewing suppliers*
Web design companies are now proliferating at great speed,
and this makes life easier for new people. You will encounter
a lot of jargon, but don't be led astray: it is perfectly
acceptable to ask exactly what somebody means in simple
terms, and if they cannot explain it to you simply and clearly,
they probably don't know what they are talking about.

*Appointing a 'Webmaster'*
One of the best bits of jargon is 'Webmaster'. The
Webmaster is responsible for the Web site, and the
Webmaster is currently you! Would you like to continue in
this role? Is this the best use of your time? Do you need to
recruit somebody from outside, from a computing,
communications, sales or design background? Or should
they be a combination of all four, or even a leader of an
Internet team of 10 people? Establishing the right resources
for the task is key.

The 'Webmaster' is normally responsible for:

- The accuracy of the site content
- Ensuring all information is up to date
- Receiving and distributing feedback and enquiries (this
  can be done through direct e-mail links)
- Managing development of the site

Having decided who will be Webmaster, and having reviewed their resources and responsibilities, you should be in a position to decide if you will undertake the design of the site yourself, or if you will put the task out to a third party.

*Choosing a supplier*

If you do not feel confident to undertake the necessary programming and development yourself, some form of external supplier will be required. There are many different kinds of companies who could help you in this area, design companies, computer companies and even a new breed of 'Web' companies. The latter are likely to be most technically competent but will not necessarily be the best overall, since design is also important. Certainly, developing Web sites has become a major growth industry, and you do need to go through a careful process to get a company that will be right for you.

When reviewing possible suppliers, you need to:

- Ask them to give you the URLs of Web sites they have already designed
- Take up references at some companies they have delivered Web sites for
- Ask if they can help with updating the site
- Find out whom they recommend as Web hosts, or see if they will host the site themselves
- Ask about site marketing services – how can they help here?

There is a whole world of strategy involved in the marketing of Web sites, such as the example given earlier in the week where the first 50 words of your site are used to attract search engines. Does your prospective supplier have skills in this important area? Can they organise for you to be registered in your preferred categories with all the relevant search engines, and what would this service cost?

The three key resources you will need are:

1 technical competence
2 graphics design flair
3 a quality writing style

Do you have these skills inside your own organisation? Often, you find that your own computer people love the Internet and will be able to help you a great deal. Explain what your objectives are, involve them in the planning process and gather their ideas. But make sure you are in the driving seat. Imagine they are printing your brochure. Don't let them design the Web site for you, and make sure they do deliver exactly what was agreed. One of the reasons computers are often difficult to use is that technical people have traditionally developed the software. Now it is your turn.

*Action point*
As we keep saying, the key mindset is to think of the user. Put yourself in the position of someone who is just starting out on the Web and has arrived at your site. Be simple and clear in navigation and communication. Assume nothing, and help them through.

*Teamworking*
The very best Web sites are the result of very close co-operation between designers and programmers. Some people manage to combine these two skills, but this is an extremely rare talent which more people claim to have than actually do have.

Be very cautious about your own skills as a designer. Certain principles apply, like less is more, and don't make everything illegible with a busy repeat pattern in the background. Whatever happens, don't try to reinvent yourself as a designer if you are not trained in this role. Use people who are skilled in the areas you want to develop.

The best design looks simple, but it can take a genius to make something very very simple.

As you work through the graphical aspects of the site, pay attention to the nitty gritty. Namely:

*Sequencing data*
Try to make sure that information downloads in the most effective order so that users are reading impactful text immediately while the graphics begin to download, rather than staring at an empty screen and twiddling their thumbs.

*Graphics*
You should be aware that graphics are so time-consuming to download that some people configure their browsers to not actually show any graphics at all and show only text. If you want to catch these people too, you will need to test out your site designs to check they work well both with and without graphics.

If you wish to achieve some elaborate effect such as creating a 'three-dimensional world' which visitors to your site can intuitively click their way through, you will need to seek professional advice!

*Digital photography*
Some aspects of graphics are very easy to organise. If you have a digital camera, you can take pictures and feed them directly into your Web site without the need for film, processing or scanning. This could be a real boon for people selling cars or houses who have a regular need for film.

*Developing complex functions*

To undertake the rapid exchange of information and the calculation required for building up shopping lists or completing forms, you will need small programs running on the server, like CGI (common gateway interface) scripts. To write these in computer code requires some considerable competence. There are, however, some existing systems you can buy which automatically create this functionality, although they may only be compatible with one particular Web-hosting company.

*Putting your site on the Internet*

Unless you go to the extraordinarily expensive and complex lengths of connecting directly into the Internet, you will need an Internet Service Provider (or ISP) to host your site for you. Selecting the right company to host your Web site is an important decision. You need to check that they are going to be the right people for you to work with, ideally for many years.

Start by planning what you are going to require for the year, and also think what lies beyond that horizon:

- Will you need to update the site every month, week or day?
- Will you be able to update it remotely over the Internet?
- What information can your Web site hosting service provide for you regarding site traffic?
- How big will your site be? What data file size?
- What programs are available on the host's servers (search, feedback, shopping list etc.)?

## Questions to ask prospective suppliers

When you have narrowed down the field, you need to specifically question prospective providers to make sure:

- They are up to the job
- They are right for you

It is fair to say that in any new industry, it is hard to sift out the really good companies from the not-so-right companies. Part of the joy of the Internet is the infinite variety of people involved in it. One of the problems is to find the right people when you need help. Specific questions to ask prospective suppliers include:

- Are they a big company, like BT, or someone you have never heard of?
- How long have they been trading?
- How good is their equipment, and can they cope?
- Do they keep an access log of all visitors' domain names and the pages they accessed, and is it split by particular day?

- Can they provide you with detailed analysis regarding the 'hit' rate on different areas of your site?
- How many visits can they cope with?
- How often does your Web host back up the information they hold to avoid the risk of its being lost?

Of course, the main question is: what does the service cost? This too can be very difficult to calculate and compare:

- Is there a set price for a complete 'package' service?
- What storage capacity is offered for what price?
- What is the limit to hits, and how much does it cost to exceed the limit?
- Do they charge by throughput (i.e. by how much is downloaded)?
- Will they register your domain name for you?
- Does the total include an e-mail account?

*Action point*
The above lists of considerations seem very complex but they are not. If you are uncertain, ask to contact any customer they have had for one year or more. Decide if you trust them. Try to judge if they have a clear and honest charging policy. If you are in any doubt, go with a well-known brand where you can – if necessary – demand a quality service.

Don't make any hasty decision when it comes to making an appointment. You need to be absolutely sure that the people you choose can do what you want them to.

## Summary

The Internet is a strange and wonderful thing. Be prepared to face unprecedented demands on your time. Maybe you will have to read millions of e-mails from students in Canada or Japan! Maybe you will have to fulfil bulk orders to France. Either way, prepare for significant challenges, and expect the unexpected.

By the end of today, you should have defined the resources you require to effectively undertake the work. Finding time to use the medium could well be the biggest challenge. Try to build this fact into your resource plan. You should also have set a clearly defined and achievable timetable for the delivery of the site.

Remember, Web technology is changing almost every week. To avoid getting your fingers burnt, go with proven technology and try to avoid anything too complex early on. Sticking with the herd has a lot going for it.

# The detailed work

Today is the day to start detailed work on the site – to start getting it up and running. The three main elements here are design, copywriting and programming.

## Design

This is key because the Web is a graphical medium and a good graphic designer should be the visual editor of your whole Internet communication. The structuring process has already been described, so make sure the navigation principles you have developed are carried through effectively into the design process. For example, if you have four main areas to a site, should you use colour coding to help the user understand immediately exactly where they are?

Good design is about the brain and the eye. Don't let the limited freedom of the computer screen extinguish your early inspiration. Just as if you were developing a magazine or brochure, slowly work towards establishing a design 'grid'. However, it is vital to also make sure that on every page, navigation is clear and easy to use, and that the 'journey' the new user takes is at the front of your mind. Refer to notes you made from an early review of sites, and try to match the best examples.

When you consider imagery, assess all the copyright-free images you own. Which ones would be most appropriate to use on the site? Put them in sample positions and look to see how they feel. Next, scan these images into your computer and see how they look and feel on screen.

Look through your existing literature and advertising to see what images you have available for use on the site. Do also check that you have the rights to use images on the Web as you may have only purchased use for print. If there is nothing suitable, you could try purchasing a CD-ROM of copyright-free images. Most Web-design companies should have stocks of these.

*Design guidelines*
If you work in a large company, the design process must begin by referring to the corporate design guidelines. These are extremely important because you are bumper to bumper with all the other parts of your organisation. In the physical world, you will be 18,000 km from your sister company in Australia. On the Internet, you are next door. Failure to look coherent with reference to them will give people the impression that you are fragmented, confused and disorganised.

If your company does not have corporate design guidelines for Internet communications, contact head office straight away. This could be your chance to save the company from looking awful. If you are at head office, make sure you implement consistent corporate design guidelines straight away. The beauty of design guidelines is that everything looks completely consistent, and you only pay once for the template.

*Test how it looks as you go*
Try to test each design concept and image viewed by using at least two different browsers on an old and a new machine. How does it look on a low-specification machine? How can the palette of colours be made to work most effectively? How can the text be made more legible? There

is a technique for this called 'anti-aliasing'. Always test the design work against both a high-quality machine and a low-quality one. Issues relating to achieving fidelity of colour most often ruin the look and feel of Internet sites. Take time to get this area right.

*Developing a prototype*

As early as possible in the development process, a full prototype should be developed in HTML to show the home page and some basic navigation. At the first opportunity, this should be shown to colleagues and ideally customers and friends to find out:

- Are the headings clear?
- Is the text legible?
- Do the graphics add to the communication?
- Is it enjoyable to use?

You also need to remember the key communications issues which were in your mind when you began developing your site. Make sure the design effectively answers the following key questions:

- What were the original objectives for the site?
- Why does this site meet those objectives?
- Whom is the site aimed at?
- How well does it communicate with them?
- Where is there room for improvement?
- When will you know you have the right design?

## Writing for Web sites

Writing for Web sites is a new science – or should that be Black Art? In many ways, it requires a new set of rules. It is undoubtedly true that over the coming years the skills of writing for the Web will be sharpened and honed by those in the industry. At present, much of the writing is embarrassingly amateur. It is equally true that the writing of Web sites needs to be taken away from the techies and

beaurocrats who so frequently seem to have control of this area. These people tend to swamp the site with detail and to write in quite traditional – not to say unintelligible – ways.

The unique nature of the Web means there are special demands involved in writing for it. For a start, the Web is truly interactive. It thrives on users feeling involved and part of the process. So dry, one-dimensional text just won't wash. Also, some companies have simply taken their printed material and put it on their Web site. This is a mistake because it feels flat and stiff to users who will quickly move to a site specifically written with the new reality in mind. It is a mistake also because, technically, the written page is generally bigger than a Web screen, and this means you get Web pages swimming with too much text. If you look at Web sites that are easy to navigate, the text tends to be shorter and more bespoke. With Web sites you therefore need to write to this new and different format. In addition, because the idea of the Internet is that it offers an information-rich medium, there is a premium on, and an attractiveness to, brevity. And furthermore, the Internet is truly international, so beware of using language that excludes others. Many users will not have English as a first language. They will struggle with jargon and obscure English even more than will a native speaker.

However, although there is much talk of the need for new approaches to writing, some of the old values still hold true. The writing itself needs to be clear and precise. It needs to have the end-user in mind too. The most important thing to remember is that people graze on Web sites. They will give you just a few seconds before they make up their mind whether to stick with you. A jumble of hard-to-read text will mean your Web site fails. They stay as long as they are interested. So your written style needs to be short and punchy.

A common mistake of the Internet is to be irritatingly obscure in an attempt to be 'groovy'. This frankly mad style of writing is more likely to irritate than to amuse. You don't need a pony tail and a brain transplant to write for the Web – just a nice way with words and a feel for the audience. If you can inhabit the experience of users, then your writing is likely to work for them.

Let's take an example. You might have two sections of your site, one selling cars and the other selling car parts. It is better to call them 'Cars for sale' and 'Car parts list' respectively rather than 'Wheel deals' and 'Wheel pieces' – we'd plump for the former rather than the latter. If you give buttons obscure titles, people may well lose patience and interest.

Whatever you do, test out your written style to make sure it grabs people's attention.

Surfing the Net is very frustrating. You wait ages to download a page, and then it is often rubbish. The key is to make yours worthwhile through the use of language that is genuinely fit for the purpose. Just putting existing material on your site is unlikely to work.

## Programming

This area is where all your previous efforts will succeed or fail. You need to be sure that the original designs and prototype are developed into a Web site where attention to detail triumphs over speed and inexperience!

If you do decide to do it yourself, you will need to use one or more Web-site construction programs which will create pages for you in HTML, the Internet programming language. It is possible to code pages in HTML directly, but new software shows that this is really a laborious and unnecessary way to proceed. The coding of HTML can even be done inside later versions of the main browsers.

HTML continues to evolve, offering – in conjunction with the latest browsers – an endless and expanding range of design possibilities. However, we again strongly recommend that you test that your site works well on a low-specification machine with a slow modem and an old browser, because that is what a lot of people have still got.

Simple programs such as Microsoft FrontPage 97 are available, but there are also more specialist packages. If you are short of money, try AOLpress which is downloadable to all for free even if you are not a member of AOL; find it at 'http://www.aol.com'. Some programs include professionally designed templates for Web pages. For Apple Macs, try programs such as Adobe PageMill. There are some interesting new technologies such as Shockwave and Flash from Macromedia. Shockwave is a system for sending Macromind Director files across the Internet. Flash is a vector-based system allowing simple graphics to download at a phenomenal speed.

We must stress it is necessary to read a variety of recent reviews before pursuing any of these avenues. If you are in any doubt whatsoever, don't do anything complicated. Take advice from reputable software sales outlets regarding the level of experience required to master these new products.

If you have the latest version of a major word-processing package, you may find it already offers the opportunity to save files directly into HTML. However, for the range of tasks necessary to construct a Web site, for the next couple of years you will probably need a Web page editor program.

Make sure that links are clearly visible against the background colour. Ensure that your colour choice is compatible with a maximum of 256 colours, as this is how the majority of computers will display the page. There are many complex technical issues relating to colour and palettes. Make sure you are familiar with these, and during the development process, always check the finished site on a variety of different specification machines with at least two types of browser. Animated graphics and 'blinking' links can cause an unfortunate delay in downloading. Avoid them if the file size is too large.

Ensure also that the page size does not exceed the size of the typical browse window.

*Action point*
The area of programming is key in two ways. First, small mistakes can cause major failures or even the collapse of the whole site. Second, there is a tremendous potential to excel in this new medium simply by doing well, because many other people simply don't bother. If you imagine your letterhead or business card was printed with a blemish, spot or other imperfection, would that be acceptable to you? Treat your Internet communications with the same respect.

*Creating a great site*
We have talked a lot about technical issues and best practice in terms of the business process. But there is another side to communications which is just as important. This is all about using art, wit, humour and plain old human ingenuity to produce a Web site which captures the imagination,

entertains, informs and adds value to the users' experience. Part of the trick here is to take the best features from conventional media and combine these with the limitless potential of interactivity. Here are some ideas:

- Include an electronic quiz, a calculator function or some other interactive tool
- Offer a downloadable screensaver or some other fun gift
- Include enormous amounts of information on your site that visitors can search electronically
- Customise your Web site for each visitor, let them state their preferences and then automatically construct a site exactly for them

If you manage to combine some interactive features like the ones above with a good, clean, clear communications style, you should end up with a great Web site.

*Action point*
Keep the design clear, use interactivity, make sure the information is well-structured and use simple navigation. If you follow these main principles, you won't go far wrong.

## Summary

By the end of today, you should have finished allocating information to particular sections, developed basic designs and tested them with some potential users. In addition, the written style for the site will have been established and the programming will have begun. You should be well on your way to developing a great site, and so take time to check this emerging new site against your original objectives.

# Testing and launching the site

The challenge today is to make sure you really do get your Web site exactly right. Don't underestimate how important this area actually is. A great communications consultant once said: 'The devil is in the detail.'

*The testing process*
Since the site development began, you have been regularly testing it against different browsers and machines. Now is the time to formalise that process and put in place some procedures to make sure it all works as well as it can.

*Progress spreadsheet*

During the site development, each section will have to go through a variety of stages. These are:

- Confirm navigation
- Allocate the copy
- Set the design style
- Assemble the images
- Enter the copy
- Proof-read the copy
- Scan in the images
- Programme the Web pages
- Check their appearance on different browsers
- Check their appearance on different machines

You may find it useful to develop a large 'Project Progress' spreadsheet showing each section of your Web site and charting its progress through each of these stages. This spreadsheet will become your core plan which can always be referred to during the development process. If you include the milestones from your timetable on the Project Progress chart, you can also use it to see if you are on schedule.

*Co-ordination with colleagues*

All successful company communications are usually the result of a team effort, but this is especially true of a Web site which can be used to communicate every aspect of your business. When work begins, you need to allocate clear responsibilities to each member of the team. Hold a meeting where a list of all the tasks is set up on the wall. See who wants to take which jobs. It is usually better if people concentrate on the area that most appeals to them.

To make sure everything is coming together at the right speed, try to hold regular progress meetings with everybody involved on the team.

The act of putting together a Web site requires high levels of project management and three verities of that said discipline, bringing the project in:

- On time
- Within the budget
- To a high enough standard of quality

We have seen Web site projects that have gone horribly over budget and over time. We have seen Web sites that must surely have disappointed the companies that produced them.

Just because Web sites are seen as arty and creative, this is no excuse to let your critical faculties go out of the window. Indeed, because the area is so new and the possibilities so enormous, someone needs to really make sure the whole project runs smoothly. This means checking regularly that the project is on course, that there are no disasters about to happen, and that if things are going wrong, there is a plan to put them right.

As we said earlier, developing a Web site can be very demanding. However, it is likely to create a lot of interest, often from the most senior people in an organisation. At every stage, therefore, it pays to make sure you are involving all key stakeholders.

*Using progress charts*
Use the Project Progress chart to check everything is going smoothly. The following are some key project questions:

- Have the navigation principles been established?
- Is the navigation structure clear and simple?
- Has the navigation structure chart been distributed to everyone and explained in detail?
- Is the copy coming together at the right speed?
- Are the images being found?
- Is the design development progressing to plan?
- Who is taking responsibility for proof-reading copy?
- Who is taking responsibility for checking the quality of images?
- Who is taking responsibility for checking the links work correctly?
- Who is taking responsibility for making sure the graphics file sizes are not too large?
- Who is taking responsibility for ensuring the site conforms to the corporate design guidelines?
- Who is taking responsibility for checking that any interactive features you have developed perform correctly?

*Action point*

As you develop the Web site project, some tasks will be
able to progress independently of one another, whereas
others will be dependent on completing one area before
moving on to the next. The sequence of tasks which depend
on each other is called the 'critical path' of the project. As
co-ordinator of the team, your responsibility is to make
sure the critical path is not interrupted, as this will make
the whole project late.

*Sign-off procedures*

Anyone who has worked with a quality design or printing
company will be familiar with the idea of 'sign-off'. This
process involves the client checking artwork before it goes
to print. A final check is made of the correctness of all
information, of images and of image quality, and a very
sustained process of proof-reading is undertaken. Having
said this, there should be no mistakes found as this has all
been checked at least twice before. However, it is still

checked a final time, and the client then 'signs off' the artwork as ready for print.

These procedures were developed because an error in artwork which is printed many thousands of times can end up costing many thousands of pounds. The beauty of the Internet is that errors need not be so expensive to rectify. However, that is no excuse for accepting any reduction in the quality of communications, and you should approach your Web site with the same duty of care as you would for print.

To achieve the above, develop a 'sign-off' sheet for each page of your site. Make sure that every screen on the site has been checked for all relevant criteria of quality. And do this for at least two different browsers on two different types of machine:

- Check the text is completely legible
- Check the images look really good
- Check that the images and the whole page line up exactly to your design plan
- Check that the page file size does not exceed your target maximum, so that download time is within your target speed
- Check the text has no errors whatsoever
- Check that each HyperText link away from the page works correctly
- Check that the navigation works correctly, linking back up to home page etc.
- Check that the interactive functions perform correctly

When all of this has been completed, you can then 'sign off' that page as ready to be posted to the Internet.

*Action point*
The Project Progress chart and screen sign-off sheets will provide you with a detailed record of the way your Web site has developed. They will help to make everyone involved aware of each other's progress and they will give authority to quality control. Using clear project-management tools will allow your team to produce an excellent, quality product first time.

## Launching the site

Once your whole Web site is ready to post to the Internet, you should hand it over to your hosting service. As soon as the site is available on the Public Internet, ask them to telephone you. Immediately check that the site matches exactly the quality and performance established at the sign-off stage. You will have set a maximum file size to ensure acceptable download speed. Check the pages are loading sufficiently quickly.

If you wish to include a larger audience in this testing stage, ask your Web-hosting company to post the site in a password-protected area. You can then let a wide group of suppliers, customers and friends view your site and give feedback before publicly posting it to the Internet.

Now, if you are completely happy with the site, you must let the world know about it! After all, isn't it a great opportunity to get back in contact with all your past and possible customers to let them know the good news!

*Publicity*

There are a number of different ways to highlight your Web site, but the immediate procedure should be as follows:

- Write to all your clients, suppliers and friends
- Add your Web address to your letterhead, business cards and brochures
- Make sure your Web address appears on all your advertising (it is normally adequate to write 'www.xyz.co.uk' rather than the whole URL beginning 'http:// ... '
- Register with all the main Internet search engines
- Begin to establish links with other sites

And the publicity should be ongoing. You've created this great organic, developing Web site, so keep people up to date with developments on it. It is a sad fact that a great proportion of Web sites become 'cobwebbed' (see page 12). These dormant sites clog up and slow down the Web and are clearly a sad waste of time and effort for those who developed the sites. So the message is: keep your Web site live and keep it publicised. If you yourself don't show enthusiasm for the site, how do you expect the users to?

## Summary

By the end of today, you should have established the systems for managing site development, built the site in full, checked every single aspect of the site, posted it to the Internet and begun to publicise it to the world.

For some companies, the work you have done today takes
a few months! However, because you have planned
correctly and are using all the right procedures, we are sure
it won't take you too long. Getting it right is the most
important thing.

# Further possibilities

The weekend is here at last after the most hectic week. Today is the day to get up late, have a cup of coffee, pat yourself on the back and think a bit more strategically about the future of your Internet presence. Although the week has involved you in a lot of action, there still needs to be time for contemplation.

You might also like to spend some time dreaming some dreams about this truly mind-blowing communications medium, and where it will eventually take you.

## Dreams, dreams, dreams

We all dream – some in colour, some in black-and-white. What makes Web sites so amazing is that they can act as the focus for our dreams – after all, they help us to plug into the whole world of information. Today you should clear some space for yourself and have a pen and paper handy. Jot down all your dreams about the Web site you have created and what role you think it will have for you and your organisation in the future. Don't limit yourself in any way. You've done the hard work so enjoy having some time to think through what might be possible – what might happen.

The following are just a selection of dreams to dream. You will, no doubt, come up with many of your own.

*Designing millions of pages or just one?*
For large Web sites, it clearly makes no sense whatsoever to have page after page of information in HTML. It will be infinitely quicker, easier and better to keep all your information on a central database in some form of common database format. This can then be combined with good database software to generate new Web pages automatically, as they are accessed. This is sometimes referred to as developing Web pages 'on the fly'. The beauty of this system is that you can achieve absolute consistency in the grid and format of information. This makes life much easier for the user. Another advantage of using this system is that you can, if you wish, change the design of the whole site by simply altering one template. This is clearly the future direction for all large Web sites.

It is both desirable and necessary for head office to take an overview of the Web sites of all parts of the company. This is because they should all be linked together with all your other offices and sites, thereby maximising the opportunities to cross-sell products and services across divisions and regions.

*Managing the site long-term*

What should be the resources for site maintenance? Who is going to be responsible for the task? You, a colleague, or a supplier? To what programme, schedule and plan will they be working?

*Electronic commerce*

'Electronic commerce' is the name commonly given to the next phase of Internet development. Essentially, there are very many things which could be achieved here, including selling goods and services over the Web. If you are considering this area, it is good to consider the following:

- distribution: how can you deliver globally?
- product differences: is what you sell the same in every country?
- price differences: does it cost the same in every country?

If you do go down this road, you will also probably want to link your back-office systems with your Web site so that customers can see the status of their orders. All of this will require planning.

*Linking databases*

If you have a large product range, would it be best for people to access information directly from your central database? If this is the case, you will have to establish a special link with your Internet Service Provider, or perhaps even consider hosting the Internet site yourself – although this would involve another level of spending. If this is your approach, how can you avoid 'hackers' breaking into your company's computers? To do this, you will need to establish an unbreakable gateway which is called a 'Firewall'.

*Global business development*

The potential of electronic commerce is truly mind-boggling. In the last year, General Electric of the USA purchased $1 billion worth of goods and services over the Net. Each supplier sees exactly the same information and bids for contracts on a global basis. Consider how your Web site might fit into this new world. Will you want to buy, sell or trade over the Internet? Perhaps you want to do all three!

The Dell computer corporation sells over $1 million of merchandise per day over the Net. In the business-to-business environment, money need not change hands. Traditional, vetted customers place orders delivered to known addresses, and the potential for fraud is minimised. Negotiated discounts can be automatically calculated.

If you use a database, customers can search for information about just those products they are interested in. Some companies have even written special software so you can pick and choose your own configuration, and the Web site calculates the price automatically!

*Collaboration with your customers*
If collaboration with your audience is important, would it be sensible to consider hosting 'chatrooms' where people can discuss topics? These facilities would again require closer collaboration with your Internet Service Provider (or ISP) but could provide a real way to add value to a visit to your site. These forums tend to require some form of 'editor' or 'moderator', so you could take that role for yourself, if you have the time.

*'Push' technology*
Further ahead, you should consider the most striking new development in Web technology called 'push'. This is really something new. The idea is simple: ask users who visit your site to request information that interests them. Having gathered their details, you then use Internet technology to

send them whatever they have asked for, either monthly, or daily, or hourly! 'Push' technology turns every publisher into a broadcaster. The most successful services utilise a computer screensaver to run headlines past the user when they are sitting and chatting. To review 'push' technology properly, check out the leader in the field at: 'http://www.pointcast.com'.

*Business strategies*
How can you make money over the Internet? If your business does not require delivery of physical goods, it is possible to develop an Internet strategy which involves offering what you do for a couple of weeks for free. This kind of lateral-thinking approach is the best way to hook customers. This is a new medium, and you need to be inventive. Having said that, you may want to avoid undermining the integrity of your existing communications channels by giving free information over the Web. The balance may be hard to find.

*What lies ahead?*
It is extremely difficult to predict the future of technology, and it is a fool who tries, but some trends seem likely. First, expect a greater proliferation of electronic payment systems, chip cards and other new kinds of charge-up cards. These will all make it even easier to shop on-line. Also, expect PC-based video-conference systems to proliferate. Soon your Web site may be a vehicle for initiating a video telephone conversation with a customer, supplier or friend. When this becomes commonplace, the retail opportunities can only be guessed at.

*Are there ethical issues?*
It seems inevitable that for the immediate future, the Internet

will seriously uproot much existing business and may result in a lot of unemployment. On this difficult note, we would like to end this book. As you look further ahead, consider the prospect that the economy might grow without creating jobs. We would all do well to spend time thinking of alternative options to the current financial system. Business is wonderful and will always meet most of our needs. However, we should recognise that business is not designed to pay for much urgent work that needs to be done in society, and it may fail to provide the large number of jobs it used to because so much work will be done by machines.

Regarding the environment, the Internet offers wonderful opportunities but also some threats. Clearly, Internet communications use very little energy and are far more environmentally responsible than creating paper and shifting it around the world. However, the escalating globalisation of the marketplace may result in massive increases in energy-intensive imports and exports. Sustainable development is in the whole world's interests.

## A final thought

A great economist once said it is better to export recipes than cakes. Information is what the Internet is best at communicating, so cook up a Web site for the world!

**Further** *Successful Business in a Week* **titles from Hodder & Stoughton and the Institute of Management all at £6.99**

| | | |
|---|---|---|
| 0 340 60896 X | Appraisals in a Week | ☐ |
| 0 340 70546 9 | Assertiveness in a Week | ☐ |
| 0 340 57640 5 | Budgeting in a Week | ☐ |
| 0 340 67009 6 | Business Plans in a Week | ☐ |
| 0 340 59813 1 | Business Writing in a Week | ☐ |
| 0 340 68002 4 | Communication at Work in a Week | ☐ |
| 0 340 62032 3 | Computing for Business in a Week | ☐ |
| 0 340 62740 9 | Customer Care in a Week | ☐ |
| 0 340 70543 4 | CVs in a Week | ☐ |
| 0 340 63154 6 | Decision Making in a Week | ☐ |
| 0 340 62741 7 | Direct Mail in a Week | ☐ |
| 0 340 64330 7 | Empowerment in a Week | ☐ |
| 0 340 66374 X | Environmental Management in a Week | ☐ |
| 0 340 59856 5 | Finance for Non-Financial Managers in a Week | ☐ |
| 0 340 67925 5 | Fundraising and Sponsorship in a Week | ☐ |
| 0 340 66375 8 | Going Freelance in a Week | ☐ |
| 0 340 65487 2 | Human Resource Management in a Week | ☐ |
| 0 340 59812 3 | Interviewing in a Week | ☐ |
| 0 340 63152 X | Introducing Management in a Week | ☐ |
| 0 340 62742 5 | Introduction to Bookkeeping and Accounting in a Week | ☐ |
| 0 340 60895 1 | Leadership in a Week | ☐ |
| 0 340 65503 8 | Managing Change in a Week | ☐ |
| 0 340 63153 8 | Managing Information in a Week | ☐ |
| 0 340 70537 X | Marketing in a Week | ☐ |
| 0 340 67924 7 | Marketing Plans in a Week | ☐ |
| 0 340 57466 6 | Market Research in a Week | ☐ |
| 0 340 60894 3 | Meetings in a Week | ☐ |
| 0 340 61137 5 | Mentoring in a Week | ☐ |
| 0 340 57522 0 | Motivation in a Week | ☐ |
| 0 340 70545 0 | Negotiating in a Week | ☐ |
| 0 340 64341 2 | Networking in a Week | ☐ |
| 0 340 67922 0 | Planning for Retirement in a Week | ☐ |
| 0 340 70541 8 | Planning Your Own Career in a Week | ☐ |
| 0 340 70544 2 | Presentation in a Week | ☐ |
| 0 340 65563 1 | Process Management in a Week | ☐ |
| 0 340 70539 6 | Project Management in a Week | ☐ |
| 0 340 64761 2 | Problem Solving in a Week | ☐ |
| 0 340 56479 2 | Public Relations in a Week | ☐ |
| 0 340 62738 7 | Purchasing in a Week | ☐ |
| 0 340 67923 9 | Report Writing in a Week | ☐ |
| 0 340 70538 8 | Selling in a Week | ☐ |
| 0 340 67397 4 | Selling on the Internet in a Week | ☐ |
| 0340 57889 0 | Stress Management in a Week | ☐ |
| 0 340 70542 6 | Succeeding at Interviews in a Week | ☐ |
| 0 340 64342 0 | Teambuilding in a Week | ☐ |
| 0 340 70547 7 | Time Management in a Week | ☐ |
| 0 340 61889 2 | Training in a Week | ☐ |
| 0 340 66935 7 | Understanding Benchmarking in a Week | ☐ |
| 0 340 70540 X | Understanding Business on the Internet in a Week | ☐ |
| 0 340 62103 6 | Understanding Business Process Re-engineering in a Week | ☐ |
| 0 340 56850 X | Understanding Just in Time in a Week | ☐ |
| 0 340 71174 4 | Understanding Mind Maps® in a Week | ☐ |
| 0 340 61888 4 | Understanding Quality Management Standards in a Week | ☐ |
| 0 340 65504 6 | Understanding Statistics in a Week | ☐ |
| 0 340 58764 4 | Understanding Total Quality Management in a Week | ☐ |
| 0 340 62102 8 | Understanding VAT in a Week | ☐ |
| 0 340 67905 0 | Understanding Virtual Organisation in a Week | ☐ |
| 0 340 70508 6 | Web Sites in a Week | ☐ |

*All Hodder & Stoughton books are available from your local bookshop or can be ordered direct from the publisher. Just tick the titles you want and fill in the form below. Prices and availability subject to change without notice.*

To: Hodder & Stoughton Ltd, Cash Sales Department, Bookpoint, 39 Milton Park, Abingdon, Oxon, OX14 4TD. If you have a credit card you may order by telephone – 01235 400414.
E-mail address: orders@bookpoint.co.uk

Please enclose a cheque or postal order made payable to Bookpoint Ltd to the value of the cover price and allow the following for postage and packaging:
UK & BFPO: £1.00 for the first book, 50p for the second book and 30p for each additional book ordered up to a maximum charge of £3.00.
OVERSEAS & EIRE: £2.00 for the first book, £1.00 for the second book and 50p for each additional book.

Name: ...............................................................................................................................................................

Address: ...........................................................................................................................................................

..........................................................................................................................................................................

If you would prefer to pay by credit card, please complete:

Please debit my Visa/Mastercard/Diner's Card/American Express (delete as appropriate) card no:

Signature ............................................................................. Expiry Date ..................................................